Bond

STRETCH
Verbal Reasoning
Tests and Papers

8–9 years

Frances Down

Nelson Thornes

Published in 2013 by:
Nelson Thornes Ltd
Delta Place
27 Bath Road
CHELTENHAM
GL53 7TH
United Kingdom

13 14 15 16 17 / 10 9 8 7 6 5 4 3 2 1

A catalogue record for this book is available from the British Library

ISBN 978 1 4085 1871 7

Page make-up by OKS Prepress, India

Printed in China by 1010 Printing International Ltd

Introduction

What is Bond?

The Bond *Stretch* series is a new addition to the Bond range of assessment papers, the number one series for the 11+, selective exams and general practice. Bond *Stretch* is carefully designed to challenge above and beyond the level provided in the regular Bond assessment range.

How does this book work?

The book contains two distinct sets of papers, along with full answers and a Progress Chart.

- Focus tests, accompanied by advice and directions, are focused on particular (and age-appropriate) verbal reasoning question types encountered in the 11+ and other exams, but devised at a higher level than the standard *Assessment Papers*. Each Focus test is designed to help raise a child's skills in the question type, as well as offer plenty of practice for the necessary techniques.

- Mixed papers are full-length tests containing a full range of verbal reasoning question types. These are designed to provide rigorous practice for children working at a level higher than that required to pass the 11+ and other verbal reasoning tests.

Full answers are provided for both types of test in the middle of the book.

How much time should the tests take?

The tests are for practice and to reinforce learning, and you may wish to test exam techniques and working to a set time limit. Using the Mixed papers, we would recommend your child spends 30 minutes answering the 45 questions in each paper.

You can reduce the suggested time by five minutes to practise working at speed.

Using the Progress Chart

The Progress Chart can be used to track Focus test and Mixed paper results over time to monitor how well your child is doing and identify any repeated problems in tackling the different question types.

A B C D E F G H I J K L M N O P Q R S T U V W X Y Z

If these words are placed in alphabetical order, underline the word that comes first.

1	graph	bears	light	kings	drops
2	hairy	found	grape	every	icicle
3	solid	turns	rated	uncle	queen
4	nuts	noun	nest	name	nits
5	bark	best	bush	boot	bike

5

In each line, underline the word that has its letters in alphabetical order.

6	pink	toys	grey	fill
7	cave	back	deep	able
8	tiny	sale	best	mole
9	king	gull	need	hint
10	koala	lorry	light	rusty

> Choose a word that looks likely to work (for example, that doesn't have 'a' as a second or third letter), then check it using the alphabet above.

5

Imagine the first four letters of the alphabet are removed. Answer these questions.

> Cover the first four letters in the alphabet above and then count carefully.

11 Which would be the third letter of those left? Circle the correct letter.

F   H   I   G

12 How many letters would there be in this alphabet? Circle the correct number.

22   24   23   21

Imagine the last four letters of the alphabet are removed. Answer these questions.

13 Which would be the last letter of those left? Circle the correct letter.

V   U   X   W

14 How many letters from the end is the letter T in the new alphabet? Circle the correct number.

2   3   4   5

4

Answer these alphabet questions.

15 Which month of the year begins with the sixth letter? _____

16 Which day of the week begins with the thirteenth letter? _____

17 Which season ends with the seventh letter? _____

18 If the days of the week are put in alphabetical order, which comes first? _____

19 If the days of the week are put in alphabetical order, which comes third? _____

5

If the letters in the following words are arranged in alphabetical order, which letter comes in the middle?

> Put the letters of the word in alphabetical order, then write the middle one.

20 PLAIN   ___   **21** BASIN   ___   **22** CLOTH   ___

23 TRAPS   ___   **24** CHARM   ___

5

Underline the word in each line that uses only the first six letters of the alphabet.

25 fade   base   node   made

26 cave   gate   beef   page

27 said   back   deaf   dune

> Write the first six letters of the alphabet and then check the words in each line carefully.

Underline the word in each line that uses three vowels.

> Write down the vowels and then count how many there are in each word. Some vowels may be repeated. These should still be counted.

28 singing   hurries   bellow   matters   dances

29 basket   laughs   skated   mailed   floppy

30 mounds   nettle   finish   bottle   excited

6

Now go to the Progress Chart to record your score!   Total   30

Always read this type of question carefully, as most of them will have similar __and__ opposite options.

Underline the two words, one from each group, that are the most opposite in meaning.

Example   (dawn, <u>early</u>, wake)   (<u>late</u>, stop, sunrise)

Underline __one__ word from each group in the brackets.

1   (might, believe, <u>high</u>)   (<u>low</u>, far, even)

2   (ancient, mature, young)   (frail, weak, old)

3   (strength, feeble, nervous)   (frightened, gathering, weakness)

4   (excuse, summer, pick)   (select, winter, forgive)

5   (strange, friendly, similar)   (peculiar, even, different)

⑤ 5

Underline the two words, one from each group, that are the most similar in meaning.

Example   (race, shop, <u>start</u>)   (finish, <u>begin</u>, end)

6   (tiny, enormous, small)   (huge, brave, generous)

7   (happiness, danger, spare)   (safety, peril, grief)

8   (finish, mark, divide)   (begin, mend, end)

9   (light, night, fight)   (pale, dark, day)

10   (there, park, leave)   (depart, come, hear)

5

Underline the pair of words that are the most similar in meaning.

Example   come, go   <u>roams, wanders</u>   fear, fare

11   rock, stone   castle, path   elephant, toy

12   ugly, lazy   pretty, beautiful   fast, slow

13   lift, drop   certain, sure   laugh, cry

14   climb, descend   noon, midnight   jump, leap

15   up, down   under, beneath   in, out

More than one pair may have similar meanings. Look for the __most__ appropriate.

5

Underline the pair of words that are the most opposite in meaning.

Example   cup, mug   coffee, milk   <u>hot, cold</u>

16	silly, tired	empty, full	tea, break
17	forwards, backwards	kick, pass	famous, known
18	light, flimsy	light, pale	light, dark
19	public, private	pink, red	quick, fast
20	simple, difficult	silver, gold	hard, shiny

⬤ 5

Underline the one word in the brackets that is the most similar in meaning to the word in capitals.

Example   UNHAPPY   (unkind   death   laughter   <u>sad</u>   friendly)

Pick the <u>most</u> similar.

21	TIRED	(weedy	wanting	weary	wishing	windy)
22	STAY	(go	leave	sleep	remain	visited)
23	SPITEFUL	(kind	helpful	greasy	nasty	hilly)
24	DIVIDE	(add	take	multiply	share	sum)
25	SINGLE	(married	one	double	return	both)

⬤ 5

Underline the one word in the brackets that is the most opposite in meaning to the word in capitals.

Example   WIDE   (broad   vague   long   <u>narrow</u>   motorway)

Pick the <u>most</u> opposite.

26	PUSH	(shove	hit	lift	maul	pull)
27	BITTER	(sour	sweet	strange	squash	acid)
28	GIVE	(puff	put	tear	take	blink)
29	CALM	(peaceful	quiet	rough	change	tranquil)
30	FAIR	(utter	dark	just	right	under)

⬤ 5

Focus test 3   Sorting words

Look at these groups of words.

	A	B	C
	Towns	Days of the week	Countries

Choose the correct group for each of the words below. Write in the letter.

1 Thursday ____   Luton ____

2 Darlington ____   Sunday ____

3 Rugby ____   Brighton ____

4 Spain ____   Greece ____

5 Poland ____   Saturday ____

> Make sure you write the correct letter for each answer.

Underline the two words that are the odd ones out in the following group of words.

Example black   <u>king</u>   purple   green   <u>house</u>

> Three of the words have something in common. In the example, it is colours.

6 house   puppy   curtain   kitten   lamb

7 run   question   skip   jump   answer

8 biscuit   cake   table   engine   sandwich

9 diamond   heart   liver   kidney   ruby

10 noun   word   verb   adjective   letter

Underline the two words in each sentence that need to change places for the sentence to make sense.

Example She went to <u>letter</u> the <u>write</u>.

> Always check the sense of the sentence carefully.

11 The main rabbit ran across the baby road.

12 Morag played seek and hide with the older children.

13 Mia waited patiently to road the cross.

14 The trees fell from the leaves.

15 Do like you summer or winter best?

Fill in the crosswords so that all the given words are included. You have been given one or two letters as a clue in each crossword.

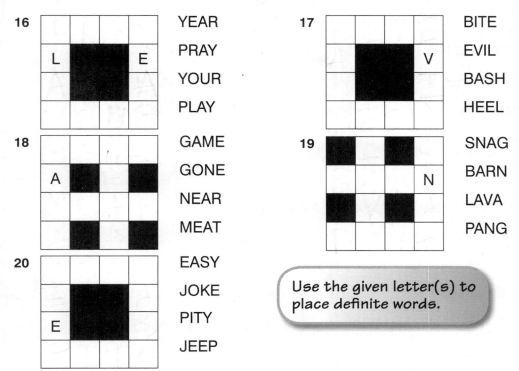

16   YEAR PRAY YOUR PLAY

17   BITE EVIL BASH HEEL

18   GAME GONE NEAR MEAT

19   SNAG BARN LAVA PANG

20   EASY JOKE PITY JEEP

> Use the given letter(s) to place definite words.

5

Rearrange the muddled words in capital letters so that each sentence makes sense.

Example   There are sixty SNODCES *seconds* in a UTMINE *minute*.

21   After CHULN _____ we had a MSUCI _____ lesson.

22   LEAPSE _____ may I sharpen my NCPIEL _____?

23   Three times ROUF _____ equals VEWTLE _____.

24   Our car did not TRAST _____ this MRNIOGN _____.

25   LDOWU _____ you like to come to my SEOUH _____?

5

Underline the two words in each line that are made from the same letters.

Example   TAP   PET   <u>TEA</u>   POT   <u>EAT</u>

26   STUD   DESK   POST   STOP   PEST

27   <u>NEST</u>   STUN   SNAP   PAST   <u>SENT</u>

28   LETS   TALE   LIST   TELL   LATE

29   LOAF   FOOL   FOAL   FEEL   LEAF

30   STUB   STEW   WENT   WEST   BEST

5

Now go to the Progress Chart to record your score!   Total   30

Focus test 4 — Selecting letters

Rearrange the muddled letters in capitals to make a proper word. The answer will complete the sentence sensibly.

Example A BEZAR is an animal with stripes.   ZEBRA

> Look at the sense of the sentence and then rearrange the letters.

1 A KCOCL tells the time.   _____

2 A RTANI runs on tracks and carries passengers.   _____

3 An CTOOPSU lives in the sea and has eight legs.   _____

4 RAFICTF lights control the vehicles on the road.   _____

5 I like TTREBU and jam on my toast.   _____

6 The boys kicked the LOAFOLBT over the fence.   _____   **6**

Which one letter can be added to the front of all of these words to make new words?

Example Care   Cat   Crate   Call   c

> Experiment with putting different letters in front of each of the words until you find the correct one.

7 __licker   __aster   __right   __arm   ____

8 __here   __rapper   __aft   __inter   ____

9 __lass   __rust   __age   __rush   ____

10 __well   __training   __peck   __hopping   ____

11 __rake   __utter   __link   __room   ____

12 __loom   __litter   __one   __utter   ____   **6**

Find the letter that will end the first word and start the second word.

Example drow (n) ought

> Look at the word on the left and find letters that could finish that word. Then see which one you can also use to start the word on the right.

13 bliste (__) ight   14 yol (__) night

10

15 clif (__) inger

16 lin (__) urtle

17 gor (__) ellow

18 bac (__) itten

6

Add one letter to the word in capital letters to make a new word. The meaning of the new word is given in the clue.

Example PLAN   simple   <u>PLAIN</u>

> Add suitable letters to the word in capitals and think about the meaning to help you. Alternatively, look at the meaning and find a word that uses the letters in capitals.

19	SON	after a short time	_____
20	URN	destroy by fire	_____
21	BUT	broken	_____
22	WORD	a weapon	_____
23	EARLY	annually	_____
24	SCAR	garment wrapped round the neck	_____

6

Remove one letter from the word in capital letters to leave a new word. The meaning of the new word is given in the clue.

Example AUNT   an insect   <u>ANT</u>

> This time, take a letter away.

25	CART	a pet animal	_____
26	FURRY	anger	_____
27	ROOT	decay	_____
28	ZONE	fewer than two	_____
29	FRAIL	don't succeed	_____
30	SHINE	front of the leg	_____

6

Focus test 5 Selecting words

Complete the following sentences by selecting the most sensible word from each group of words given in the brackets. Underline the words selected.

Example The (<u>children</u>, boxes, foxes) carried the (houses, <u>books</u>, steps) home from the (greengrocer, <u>library</u>, factory).

> Work through each sentence, bracket by bracket, choosing the most appropriate word from each one.

1 Mum (drove, ironed, caught) my (dress, cold, biscuit) really (straight, crumbly, well).

2 The (chicken, cow, sheep) from the (farm, airport, supermarket) laid brown (eggs, bread, nuts).

3 When she fell (over, by, through), she (grazed, pulled, ate) her (hair, collar, knee).

4 When the (sun, sky, rose) set behind the (curtains, hills, scene), it was suddenly (dark, light, hairy).

5 The (milk, coat, river) flowed (under, over, through) the railway (alarm, signal, bridge).

6 (Wednesday, Sunday, Tuesday) is the (month, year, day) after (Tuesday, Friday, Thursday).

Choose the word or phrase that makes each sentence true.

Example A LIBRARY always has (posters, a carpet, <u>books</u>, DVDs, stairs).

> Think about what the word in capitals <u>has</u> to have.

7 A CHAIR always has a (cushion, cover, seat, table, broken leg).

8 A POND always has (ducks, fish, weed, boats, water).

9 A TOWN always has (buildings, a station, a cinema, a park, a zoo).

10 A RABBIT always has (grass, carrots, ears, a hutch, a friend).

11 A SCHOOL always has (posters, pupils, books, a playground, a fence).

12 A WOOD always has (a stream, trees, bluebells, birds, grass).

Underline two words, one from each group, that go together to form a new word. The word in the first group always comes first.

Example (hand, <u>green</u>, for) (light, <u>house</u>, sure)

13 (work, play, day) (type, hole, <u>shop</u>)

14 (break, garden, flower) (pot, cup, mug)

15 (tall, <u>some</u>, high) (five, three, one)

16 (break, mend, spoil) (slow, fast, thing)

17 (pond, mess, dear) (park, bin, age)

18 (jump, leap, dance) (toad, frog, spring)

> Take one word at a time from the left brackets and put it in front of each of the words in the right brackets.

( ) 6

Underline the one word in each group that **cannot be made** from the letters of the word in capital letters.

Example STATIONERY stone tyres ration <u>nation</u> noisy

19 FATTEN fat ten net toe tea

20 BEETLE bet bee let tee tab

21 DRIBBLE bed bird bible drip led

22 SHADOW wash show shed dash shod

23 BRAMBLE barb mole meal mare bear

24 CABINS bins scab skin basin nibs

> Look for any letters that are not in the word in capitals, and for any repeats of letters.

( ) 6

Underline the one word in each group that **can be made** from the letters of the word in capital letters.

Example CHAMPION camping notch peach cramp <u>chimp</u>

> This time, all but one is not made from the words in capitals. Take care with vowels particularly.

25 BUZZER rub red err but use

26 DRAINS dry nap sir nod sip

27 CLEVER roe car eve eye cry

28 HANGER gain gash edge rain rage

29 WASHED show dash sawn seed ward

30 CRUMBLE crab dumb club real drum

( ) 6

Change one word so that the sentence makes sense. Underline the word you are taking out and write your new word on the line.

Example   I waited in line to buy a <u>book</u> to see the film.   <u>ticket</u>

1   Please switch on the light and draw the curtains as it is getting bright.   _____

2   The milkman delivered four pints of <u>poison</u> to our house.   _____

3   Dad bought Mum a pretty bunch of vegetables on her birthday.   _____

4   We rushed to the cinema to catch our flight to Spain.   _____

5   My mother is cooking supper in the bedroom.   _____   **5**

Find the three-letter word that can be added to the letters in capitals to make a new word. The new word will complete the sentence sensibly.

Example   The cat sprang onto the MO.   <u>USE</u>

> *Use the sense of the sentence to help you find the answer.*

6   He SPED on the ice and sprained his ankle.   _____

7   Dale's COMER crashed and he lost his work.   _____

8   Mum dropped her handbag and all the CONTS fell out.   _____

9   He tripped because his SHOELS were undone.   _____

10   In the shop, I put flour and eggs into our shopping BET.   _____   **5**

Find a word that can be put in front of each of the following words to make new, compound words.

Example   cast   fall   ward   pour   <u>down</u>

> *Look for common words such as up/down, on/in, and so on.*

11   berry   mail   smith   thorn   _____

12   room   sock   time   spread   _____

13   surfing   screen   pipe   mill   _____

14

14	house	grocer	field	finch	_____	
15	ball	step	path	bridge	_____	5

Change the first word of the third pair in the same way as the other pairs to give a new word.

Example bind, hind bare, hare but, <u>hut</u>

See how the letters have been changed, then continue the pattern. Take care with letter order.

16 fast, mast fore, more fount, _____

17 pluck, luck drain, rain swarm, _____

18 ace, pace ink, pink art, _____

19 tile, stiles lice, slices tick, _____

20 forget, get camera, era police, _____   5

Look at the first group of three words. The word in the middle has been made from the two other words. Complete the second group of three words in the same way, making a new word in the middle.

Example PA<u>IN</u> INTO T<u>OO</u>K   ALSO <u>SOON</u> ONLY

Letter by letter, see where the middle word gets its letters from. Repeat the pattern for the second group of words.

21 PARK PAST STOP   BEAK _____ ENVY

22 TINY TIDE MADE   SLIP _____ CHAP

23 CANE NEST RUST   ZONE _____ TEXT

24 PONY ONCE ICED   DARE _____ BEAN

25 QUIZ QUIT TAME   DARE _____ NOTE   5

Change the first word into the last word, by changing one letter at a time and making a new, different word in the middle.

Example CASE <u>CASH</u> LASH

26 FORM _____ HARM

27 CORN _____ BURN

28 LIKE _____ WIFE

Write down the letters that remain the same. Substitute the remaining letters one at a time.

29 HEED _____ WEEK

30 WHIP _____ SLIP   5

Now go to the Progress Chart to record your score! Total 30

If the code for FRAMES is 8 9 3 5 1 7, what are the codes for the following words?

  1 RAM _____

  2 FARM _____

  3 Using the same code, what does 7 3 5 1 stand for? _____

If the code for BUSHES is @ + × ÷ − ×, what do the following codes stand for?

  4 @ + × _____

  5 × ÷ − _____

  6 ÷ + × ÷ _____

  7 Using the same code, what is the code for USE? _____

These words have been written in code, but the codes are not written under the right words. Match the right code to each word given below.

RED	GREEN	GREY	GRASS	DRAG
F J Z M	M J H O	M J Z Q Q	M J H H P	J H F

  8 RED _____

  9 GREEN _____

  10 GREY _____

  11 GRASS _____

  12 DRAG _____

Complete the following sentences in the best way by choosing one word from each set of brackets.

Example Tall is to (tree, <u>short</u>, colour) as narrow is to (thin, white, <u>wide</u>).

> Look for the relationship between the pairs of statements. The second pairing must be completed in the same way as the first.

  13 Big is to (small, huge, far) as thin is to (fat, cold, green).

  14 Calf is to (cow, butterfly, leaf) as puppy is to (collar, dog, kitten).

  15 Hair is to (head, band, wash) as beard is to (chin, hair, curl).

  16 Rain is to (wet, drops, snow) as sun is to (warm, shine, burn).

Find the missing letters and/or numbers. The alphabet has been written out to help you.

A B C D E F G H I J K L M N O P Q R S T U V W X Y Z

Example AB is to CD as PQ is to **RS**.

> Look for the pattern. In these sequences the letters are working together. (It may help to put your finger on the alphabet line and count the number of spaces.)

17 FG is to HI as JK is to _____.

18 M9 is to N8 as O7 is to _____.

19 AC is to EG as IK is to _____.

20 ZY is to XW as VU is to _____.

4

Find the next two pairs of letters and/or numbers in the following sequences. The alphabet has been written out to help you.

A B C D E F G H I J K L M N O P Q R S T U V W X Y Z

Example CQ   DP   EQ   FP   **GQ**   **HP**

> Look for the pattern on each line. See whether the letters are working together or separately.

21 A1   B2   C3   D4   ___   ___

22 HH   II   JJ   KK   ___   ___

23 ZY   WV   TS   QP   ___   ___

24 ZD   YE   ZF   YG   ___   ___

> These letters are working separately.

25 HN   IM   JN   KM   ___   ___

26 AR   BS   CT   DU   ___   ___

6

Find the two missing numbers in the following sequences.

Example 2   4   6   8   **10**   **12**

> Look for the pattern between the numbers.

27 15   13   ___   ___   7   5

28 5   10   ___   20   ___   30

29 ___   30   27   24   21   ___

30 ___   ___   36   46   56   66

4

Now go to the Progress Chart to record your score!   Total   **30**

Focus test 8 Logic

If a = 3, b = 2, c = 4 and d = 1, what are the values of these calculations?

Replace the letters with numbers and work out the calculations.

   1 a × c = _____

   3 (a + c) − d = _____

   2 d + c + b = _____

   4 (c ÷ b) × a = _____

4

If a = 1, t = 2, e = 3, b = 4 and s = 5, what are the totals of these words?

Add each of the letter values together to make a word total.

   5 bat _____   **6** set _____   **7** best _____   **8** seat _____

4

The labrador and the poodle have green collars. The spaniel and the labrador have blue bowls. The poodle and the collie have red bowls. The collie and the spaniel have yellow collars.

Which dog has:

   9 a green collar and a red bowl?   _____

   10 a yellow collar and a blue bowl?   _____

   11 a green collar and a blue bowl?   _____

   12 a yellow collar and a red bowl?   _____

Before you start, write down the information more clearly.

4

Sarah and Jane collect coloured beads. Below is a chart of the colours they own.

	Red	Blue	Yellow	Green	Multi-coloured	Orange
Sarah	5	7	2	4	6	4
Jane	8	3	1	6	11	0

Use the information to answer the questions.

   13 How many more blue beads than Jane does Sarah have? _____

   14 Which colour bead is least popular? _____

   15 How many multi-coloured beads are there altogether? _____

   16 Who has collected the most beads? _____

4

Here is a train timetable.

CARDEN (depart)	PILLPORT (arrive)
09:50	10:35
11:20	12:05
13:50	14:35
15:20	16:05

17 How long does the journey take from Carden to Pillport? _____

18 If the 15:20 train arrived ten minutes late, what time
would I arrive at Pillport? _____

19 If I needed to be on time for an appointment in Pillport
at midday, which train should I catch from Carden? _____   3

Moira's house is opposite mine. Mine is number 13. I live on the odd side of
the road. Moira lives on the even side. There are forty houses altogether. If
number 1 is opposite number 2, number 3 is opposite 4, and so on, answer
these questions.

Before you start, work out the pattern on a piece of paper.

20 What number is opposite 6? _____

21 What is Moira's house number? _____

22 One of Moira's next-door neighbours lives at 12.
What number is her other next-door neighbour? _____

23 One of my next-door neighbours lives at number 11.
What number is my other next-door neighbour? _____

24 Lia lives opposite 38. What is her house number? _____   5

If yesterday was Thursday, answer these questions.

25 Which day of the week was it a week ago from today? _____

26 What is the day after tomorrow? _____

27 What is the day two days ago from today? _____   3

Julie has 50p more than Soo, who has 35p less than Yumi. Yumi has £1.55.
How much does each child have?

28 Soo _____   29 Julie _____

30 If Katie was 4 when her sister, Kylie, was born and she
is 9 now, how old is Kylie? _____   3

Mixed paper 1

If these words are placed in alphabetical order, underline the word that comes second.

1	ocean	stream	brook	river	sea
2	frame	garage	kangaroo	lemon	monkey
3	bird	rain	tree	salt	dare
4	pink	port	pale	peel	push
5	cage	cull	cook	cent	core

5

Find the two missing numbers in the following sequences.

Example 2   4   6   8   <u>10</u>   <u>12</u>

6	1	4	7	10	___	___
7	13	11	9	___	5	___
8	___	15	___	23	27	31
9	___	16	13	___	7	4
10	11	22	___	44	___	66

5

Change one word so that the sentence makes sense. Underline the word you are taking out and write your new word on the line.

Example I waited in line to buy a <u>book</u> to see the film.   <u>ticket</u>

11 The horse jumped across the fast-flowing river.   _____

12 During the storm, a huge branch fell off the <u>flower</u> in the park.   _____

13 The pigeon flapped its legs and flew out of the tree.   _____

14 As it has been raining so much, the pavement is really dry.   _____

15 February is the last month of the year after November.   _____

5

If a = 2, b = 4, c = 5 and d = 3, what are the values of these calculations?

16 $a + b + c + d =$ ____   **17** $c - (b \div a) =$ ____

18 $2a + 2d =$ ____   **19** $b + (c - d) =$ ____

20 $cd - b =$ ____

5

Underline the two words, one from each group, that are the most opposite in meaning.

Example   (dawn, <u>early</u>, wake)   (<u>late</u>, stop, sunrise)

21   (blue, top, simple)   (bottom, king, straight)

22   (hungry, mellow, left)   (right, wrong, black)

23   (ramble, little, huge)   (hairy, moist, large)

24   (dry, bitter, far)   (soft, part, wet)

25   (high, under, trusty)   (juicy, low, more)

5

Complete the following sentences by selecting the most sensible word from each group of words given in the brackets. Underline the words selected.

Example   The (<u>children</u>, boxes, foxes) carried the (houses, <u>books</u>, steps) home from the (greengrocer, <u>library</u>, factory).

26   The (elephants, parents, books) pushed their (letters, jellies, babies) through the park in their (prams, trees, bicycles).

27   Our (garage, hospital, shop) has lots of (cars, sweets, nurses) and doctors on (duty, rocks, rails).

28   Huw ate all the (biscuits, nails, daffodils) on the (desk, telephone, plate) on the kitchen (path, sink, table).

29   We crossed the (desert, road, river) on a (boat, pen, paper) to the other (person, side, book).

30   My (dog, door, mother) baked a delicious (cake, jacket, toast) for (afternoon, tea, meal).

5

Look at these groups of words.

1	2	3
Homes	Animals	Parts of the body

Choose the correct group for each of the words below. Write in the number.

31   castle   ____   toes   ____

32   squirrel ____   gorilla ____

33   cottage ____   palace ____

34   buffalo ____   bungalow ____

35   head   ____   leg   ____

5

Rearrange the muddled letters in capitals to make a proper word. The answer will complete the sentence sensibly.

Example   A BEZAR is an animal with stripes.   <u>ZEBRA</u>

36 Bicycles have two HELSEW and a saddle.   _____

37 That sports car has a powerful NEGNIE.   _____

38 Spiders have IGHET legs.   _____

39 I have sixteen coloured CLSIPNE on my desk.   _____

40 Jez made a delicious MELON meringue pie.   _____   **5**

Underline the one word in the brackets that is the most similar in meaning to the word in capitals.

Example   UNHAPPY   (unkind   death   laughter   <u>sad</u>   friendly)

41 DULL   (bright   sunny   cold   boring   full)

42 EDGE   (boarder   calm   hog   claim   border)

43 AMUSE   (bore   distant   entertain   thank   close)

44 CORRECT   (accurate   wrong   obvious   clear   bend)

45 FIT   (puzzle   climb   healthy   mind   brainy)   **5**

Mixed paper 2

Which one letter can be added to the front of all of these words to make new words?

Example	_C_are	_C_at	_C_rate	_C_all	_C_
1	__loud	__round	__board	__rise	____
2	__pot	__tool	__pill	__team	____
3	__lock	__hunk	__rack	__lamp	____
4	__rasp	__lint	__rate	__ape	____
5	__layer	__ear	__luck	__out	____

5

Find the three-letter word that can be added to the letters in capitals to make a new word. The new word will complete the sentence sensibly.

Example   The cat sprang onto the MO.   <u>USE</u>

6   The bell CED the hour.   _____

7   Deer like to hide among the trees in the EST.   _____

8   Hamid was LING excited about going ice
    skating for his birthday.   _____

9   A PEL has just arrived from Canada.   _____

10   There are two NIS courts in the park.   _____

5

Underline the two words that are the odd ones out in the following group of words.

Example	black	<u>king</u>	purple	green	<u>house</u>
11	glass	window	plate	tumbler	beaker
12	tiger	lion	basket	leopard	foot
13	hit	sit	punch	stand	thump
14	hockey	juice	tennis	cricket	fly
15	ring	platinum	gold	silver	service

5

23

If the code for THAMES is 5 7 3 4 1 2, what do the following codes stand for?

16 5 3 4 1   _____

17 4 3 2 5   _____

18 5 7 1 4   _____

Using the same code, what are the codes for the following words?

19 STEM   _____

20 HATE   _____

In each line, underline the word that has its letters in alphabetical order.

21	verbs	quick	koala	sorry	first
22	built	billow	guess	trunk	hunch
23	goose	crisp	berry	house	lemon
24	north	delta	horse	chimp	blast
25	shirt	mouse	boost	straw	plant

Underline the pair of words that are the most similar in meaning.

Example   come, go   <u>roams, wanders</u>   fear, fare

26 skinny, thin   bright, dull   in, out

27 sink, swim   quick, fast   likely, unlikely

28 year, day   time, space   flat, even

29 pretty, ugly   sleepy, awake   beautiful, attractive

30 weak, feeble   strong, safe   there, their

Choose the word or phrase that makes each sentence true.

Example   A LIBRARY always has (posters, a carpet, <u>books</u>, DVDs, stairs).

31 A WINDOW always has (curtains, dirt, glass, doors, a blind).

32 A CAKE always has (candles, icing, a plate, a filling, ingredients).

33 HANDS always have (gloves, fingers, rings, writing, shakes).

34 A PEACH always has a (bowl, red skin, cream, <u>stone</u>, tin).

35 A HORSE always has (hooves, a bridle, a stable, a rider, a field).

If $b = 1$, $r = 5$, $e = 2$, $a = 6$ and $d = 4$, what are the totals of these words?

36 bear   _____

37 area   _____

38 dear   _____

39 drab   _____

40 dread   _____

Underline the one word in each group that **can be made** from the letters of the word in capital letters.

Example   CHAMPION   camping   notch   peach   cramp   <u>chimp</u>

41 BASKET   tusk   skip   base   kite   boat

42 HUNGER   hang   grey   rein   rung   hurl

43 SNACKS   nose   cane   skin   scan   sock

44 FLURRY   rule   fury   your   lorry   ruff

45 BISCUIT   spurt   stick   stuck   stubs   suit

Mixed paper 3

Find the letter that will end the first word and start the second word.

Example drow (<u>n</u>) ought

1 shou (__) riplet

2 flin (__) ate

3 spi (__) ose

4 loc (__) ite

5 flas (__) oney

5

Underline the two words, one from each group, that are the most similar in meaning.

Example (race, shop, <u>start</u>)   (finish, <u>begin</u>, end)

6 (alter, same, like)   (dislike, change, loose) .

7 (heat, snow, desert)   (rain, warmth, cloud)

8 (drop, choose, mix)   (pick, hammer, spade)

9 (precious, golden, bracelet)   (valuable, rich, jewel)

10 (eager, instant, delay)   (keen, rush, hurry)

5

Find a word that can be put in front of each of the following words to make new, compound words.

Example cast   fall   ward   pour   <u>down</u>

11 teacher   boy   room   house   _____

12 man   card   mark   script   _____

13 stairs   river   on   set   _____

14 cuff   made   stand   shake   _____

15 horse   wheel   ridge   on   _____

5

Chairs A and B have flowery cushions. Chairs B and C are armchairs. Chairs A and D are ordinary chairs. Chairs D and C have plain blue cushions.

16 Which chair has flowery cushions and is an armchair?   _____

17 Which chair has blue cushions and is an ordinary chair?   _____

18 Which chair has flowery cushions and is an ordinary chair? _____

19 Which chair has blue cushions and is an armchair?   _____

4

If the letters in the following words are arranged in alphabetical order, which letter comes in the middle?

20 CABIN _____   **21** MOLES _____   **22** JOKES _____   ◯ 3

Fill in the crosswords so that all the given words are included. You have been given one letter as a clue in each crossword.

23

	■	W	■
	■		■

24

	■		N
	■		

25

	■		■
■		■	
■		■	T

FULL   FOOD   GNAT   KING   THIS   HEAP   ◯ 3
LILT   OWLS   NEAT   KILN   ECHO   POST

If the code for BRAKES is v p g d w f, what are the codes for the following words?

26 SAKE _____   **27** BARK _____   **28** KERB _____

Using the same code, what do the following codes stand for?

29 v g d w _____   **30** v w g d _____   ◯ 5

Imagine the first three letters of the alphabet are removed. Answer these questions.

A B C D E F G H I J K L M N O P Q R S T U V W X Y Z

31 Which would be the first letter of those left? Circle the correct letter.

F   D   E   C

32 Which would be the fourth letter of those left? Circle the correct letter.

H   I   G   F

33 How many letters would there be in this alphabet? Circle the correct number.

24   21   23   22

Imagine the last two letters of the alphabet are removed. Answer these questions.

34 Which would be the last letter of those left? Circle the correct letter.

V   U   X   W

35 Which letter comes halfway in the new alphabet? Circle the correct letter.

J   K   L   O

Underline the two words in each sentence that need to change places for the sentence to make sense.

Example   She went to <u>letter</u> the <u>write</u>.

36 It was watching frightening the film.

37 We hung the wall on the picture.

38 Next house we are moving week.

39 He swam very lengths of the pool four quickly.

40 We went after bed straight away to the film.

Underline two words, one from each group, that go together to form a new word. The word in the first group always comes first.

Example   (hand, <u>green</u>, for)   (light, <u>house</u>, sure)

41 (fire, sweep, clean)   (smoke, chimney, proof)

42 (scrap, end, bit)   (elbow, book, cook)

43 (van, car, for)   (sting, shine, pet)

44 (finger, bring, cushion)   (print, plant, pick)

45 (be, on, from)   (short, up, long)

Now go to the Progress Chart to record your score!   Total   45

28

Mixed paper 4

Answer these alphabet questions.

A B C D E F G H I J K L M N O P Q R S T U V W X Y Z

1 Which month of the year begins with the fourth letter? _____

2 Which day of the week begins with the sixth letter? _____

3 Which season begins with the first letter? _____

4 If the days of the week are put in alphabetical order, which comes last? _____

5 If the days of the week are put in alphabetical order, which comes fourth? _____   **5**

Add one letter to the word in capital letters to make a new word. The meaning of the new word is given in the clue.

Example PLAN   simple   <u>PLAIN</u>

6 LEVER   intelligent   _____

7 STAR   begin   _____

8 HEAT   a grain   _____

9 CREAM   shout   _____

10 SPIN   backbone   _____   **5**

Underline the one word in each group that **cannot be made** from the letters of the word in capital letters.

Example	STATIONERY	stone	tyres	ration	<u>nation</u>	noisy
11	DAMPER	pram	ramp	read	deer	pear
12	BOUNCE	bone	cone	noun	cube	once
13	GRAPES	pest	gape	sage	spar	reap
14	THORNS	sort	south	north	horn	shot
15	CARAFE	fear	fare	rice	care	face

5

Change the first word of the third pair in the same way as the other pairs to give a new word.

Example bind, hind   bare, hare   but, <u>hut</u>

16 able, table   angle, tangle   rack, _____

17 trots, rot   frame, ram   there, _____

18 wear, fear   warm, farm   wind, _____

19 swell, well   clean, lean   brain, _____

20 quick, stick   phone, stone   wheel, _____   5

Underline the pair of words that are the most opposite in meaning.

Example cup, mug   coffee, milk   <u>hot, cold</u>

21 chortle, giggle   laugh, cry   moan, complain

22 circle, ring   spotless, decent   clean, dirty

23 alive, dead   cuddle, embrace   stick, branch

24 bristly, prickly   rude, polite   bite, chew

25 begin, commence   complete, entire   tick, cross   5

If N = 5, M = 10, Q = 4, R = 3 and P = 2, what are the values of these calculations?

26 $Q + P + R + N =$ _____

27 $(M - R) - (Q - P) =$ _____

28 $(M \div N) + Q =$ _____

29 $(P \times M) \div Q =$ _____

30 $2M \div 2N =$ _____   5

Rearrange the muddled letters in capitals to make a proper word. The answer will complete the sentence sensibly.

Example A BEZAR is an animal with stripes.   <u>ZEBRA</u>

31 A RFFGIAE lives in Africa and has a very long neck.   _____

32 My dog has a smart new RCOALL round his neck.   _____

33 Six plus five equals EEENVL.   _____

34 A CDOORT makes us better when we are unwell. _____

35 TREEST is another word for a road. _____

5

Fill in the crosswords so that all the given words are included. You have been given one letter as a clue in each crossword.

36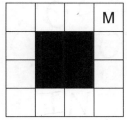

WORM

WORK

MOOD

KIND

37

LIAR

STOP

PARK

TWIN

38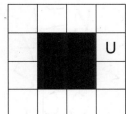

MAST

TOOK

MIND

DUSK

39

HERE

IDLE

FILL

LOVE

40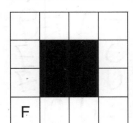

BEEF

TOUR

FOUR

BELT

5

If the code for STABLE is * ? £ > ! <, what do the following codes stand for?

41 £ > ! < _____

42 ! £ * ? _____

43 ! £ ? < _____

Using the same code, what are the codes for the following words?

44 TEAS _____

45 BEAT _____

5

Mixed paper 5

Class 1 and Class 2 counted how many children had pets. Below is a chart that shows the results.

	No pets	Dogs	Cats	Fish	Rabbits	Horses	Chickens
Class 1	4	7	8	5	3	1	2
Class 2	6	6	6	0	4	3	5

Using the information, answer the questions.

1 How many children had rabbits?   _____

2 Which was the least popular pet altogether?   _____

3 How many more chickens and rabbits did Class 2
   have than Class 1?   _____

4 How many more dogs and cats did Class 1 have
   than Class 2?   _____

5 Which class had the most types of pets owned?   _____   **5**

Rearrange the muddled words in capital letters so that each sentence makes sense.

Example   There are sixty SNODCES _seconds_ in a UTMINE _minute_.

6 We LKOEDO _____ under the rug and NDFUO _____ the
   missing puzzle piece.

7 The young soldier GHTFOU _____ bravely in the TLETBA

   _____.

8 My MTHORE _____ likes to have a vase of flowers on the

   BETAL _____.

9 Our car is RGENE _____ and lives in the RGAAEG _____
   when we are not using it.

10 My BITRAB _____ likes to leave his THUHC _____ and
    run on the lawn.   **5**

Underline the one word in the brackets that is the most similar in meaning to the word in capitals.

Example UNHAPPY (unkind   death   laughter   <u>sad</u>   friendly)

11 SIMPLE   (hard   kind   difficult   easy   reasonable)

12 CROWDED   (thin   busy   wide   early   calm)

13 FROWN   (crown   scowl   smile   <u>weep</u>   mind)

14 OLD   (early   first   frail   beneath   ancient)

15 EARN   (deserve   take   want   feel   pick)

5

Remove one letter from the word in capital letters to leave a new word. The meaning of the new word is given in the clue.

Example AUNT   an insect   <u>ANT</u>

16 ELVER   always   _____

17 POUND   small lake   _____

18 BLAME   limping   _____

19 FROCK   stone   _____

20 FRAME   celebrity   _____

5

These words have been written in code, but the codes are not written under the right words. Match the right code to each word given below.

COOK	CAVE	KICKS	COD	ASK
2 8 1 2 7	4 7 2	1 3 3 2	1 4 9 6	1 3 5

21 COOK   _____   22 CAVE   _____

23 COD   _____   24 KICKS   _____

25 ASK   _____

5

If the letters in the following words are arranged in alphabetical order, which letter comes in the middle?

26 PALMS   ____   27 YOURS   ____

28 WOMAN   ____   29 PORCH   ____

30 ARGUE   ____

5

Find the two missing numbers in the following sequences.

Example	2	4	6	8	<u>10</u>	<u>12</u>
31	8	11	__	17	20	__
32	__	88	77	66	__	44
33	1	__	5	__	9	11
34	__	__	45	40	35	30
35	17	15	__	__	9	7

5

Underline the one word in each group that **can be made** from the letters of the word in capital letters.

Example	CHAMPION	camping	notch	peach	cramp	<u>chimp</u>
36	PAUSED	days	said	soup	peas	deep
37	GLOOMY	mole	glue	loom	glow	holy
38	ICICLE	lice	iced	isle	clip	clue
39	SOOTHE	this	some	thus	sort	hose
40	QUESTS	step	sets	squat	stud	quit

5

Look at the first group of three words. The word in the middle has been made from the two other words. Complete the second group of three words in the same way, making a new word in the middle.

Example	PA<u>IN</u>	<u>IN</u>TO	<u>TO</u>OK	ALSO	<u>SOON</u>	ONLY
41	BORN	BOAT	SEAT	VEAL	_____	SPIN
42	CORE	CONE	NUMB	LADY	_____	ZIPS
43	LEAP	RULE	RUMP	REST	_____	FIND
44	DEER	WEEP	WASP	MILK	_____	FROM
45	CHAP	RICH	TRIM	THIN	_____	SPAN

5

Mixed paper 6

Underline the two words in each line that are made from the same letters.

Example TAP   PET   <u>TEA</u>   POT   <u>EAT</u>

1 LAID   SAID   DALE   SALE   DIAL

2 MARE   DEAR   ROAD   MADE   DAME

3 PORE   RODE   SORE   DOSE   ROSE

4 DUSTY   STORY   STUDY   DIRTY   TRUST

5 SPORE   SPARE   STARE   ROPES   RESTS

Cars 1 and 2 are black. Cars 3 and 4 are silver. Cars 4 and 2 have opening roofs. Cars 3 and 2 have tinted windows. Cars 1 and 4 have alloy wheels.

Which car has:

6 alloy wheels and is black? _____

7 tinted windows and an opening roof? _____

8 alloy wheels and is silver? _____

9 an opening roof and is black? _____

10 tinted windows and is silver? _____

Here is a train timetable.

| BRANWICK (depart) | 08:30 | 09:45 | 11:00 | 12:15 |
| GRANGESEA (arrive) | 09:10 | 10:25 | 11:40 | 12:55 |

11 How long does the journey take from Branwick to Grangesea? _____

12 If the 08:30 train arrived ten minutes late, what time would I arrive at Grangesea? _____

13 If I needed to be on time for an appointment in Grangesea at midday, which is the latest train I should catch from Branwick? _____

14 How many minutes are there between trains leaving Branwick? _____

15 It takes fifteen minutes to walk to the beach from Grangesea station. If I am meeting a friend there at 11:30, which train will I need to catch from Branwick? _____

Underline the word in each line that uses only the first six letters of the alphabet.

16 <u>face</u> hope gear fear

17 drop disc dent dead

18 hear corn dale bead

19 cage code cede cost

20 gate café cake good

 5

Change the first word into the last word, by changing one letter at a time and making a new, different word in the middle.

Example CASE <u>CASH</u> LASH

21 ZOOM _____ ROOF

22 BACK _____ PICK

23 HINT _____ MINK

24 BONY _____ ZONE

25 CARD _____ HAND

 5

Complete the following sentences in the best way by choosing one word from each set of brackets.

Example Tall is to (tree, <u>short</u>, colour) as narrow is to (thin, white, <u>wide</u>).

26 River is to (sea, stream, pond) as motorway is to (car, traffic, lane).

27 Grass is to (cow, field, green) as sky is to (blue, cloud, sun).

28 Happy is to (smile, amused, sad) as ugly is to (pretty, sister, odd).

29 Hand is to (finger, writing, glove) as foot is to (sock, leg, yard).

30 Station is to (train, bike, mule) as airport is to (fly, plane, runway).

 5

Fill in the crosswords so that all the given words are included. You have been given one letter as a clue in each crossword.

31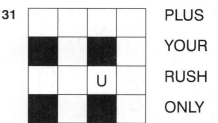

PLUS

YOUR

RUSH

ONLY

32

BOUT

THIS

KISS

BARK

 2

36

Underline the one word in the brackets that is the most opposite in meaning to the word in capitals.

Example WIDE   (broad   vague   long   <u>narrow</u>   motorway)

33 FRONT   (back   near   first   long   last)

34 CLOSE   (near   shut   related   main   open)

35 HATE   (abhor   loathe   detest   love   like)

36 NEARER   (father   away   further   beside   then)

37 BETTER   (good   best   worse   worst   bad)

5

These words have been written in code, but the codes are not written under the right words. Match the right code to each word given below.

    HURRY   HEN   NURSE   CARRY   SURE

    7 1 6 0   9 1 6 6 5   2 3 6 6 5   4 1 6 7 0   9 0 4

38 HURRY   _____

39 HEN   _____

40 NURSE   _____

41 CARRY   _____

42 SURE   _____

5

Underline the word in each line that uses three vowels.

43   hastens   harness   haircut   harvest   hatchet

44   prepare   contrast   craving   muddles   stretch

45   slapdash   elastic   skirted   crowded   skipped

3

Mixed paper 7

Look at the first group of three words. The word in the middle has been made from the two other words. Complete the second group of three words in the same way, making a new word in the middle.

Example	PAIN	INTO	TOOK	ALSO	SOON	ONLY
1	WAXY	WASH	POSH	BEND	_____	FELT
2	FLOW	WAGE	CAGE	PRIM	_____	WADE
3	COOK	WOOD	DRAW	FEEL	_____	TERM
4	MOLE	LOSE	SPUR	JIBE	_____	TEXT
5	FOUR	SOUR	SHIP	JUMP	_____	HEAD

5

Underline the two words in each sentence that need to change places for the sentence to make sense.

Example She went to <u>letter</u> the <u>write</u>.

6 The seabirds made their cliffs on the rocky nests.

7 Please close you mouth while your are chewing.

8 My chain bicycle came off this morning.

9 At twelve the clock struck midday times.

10 Why do two camels have some humps?

5

Choose the word or phrase that makes each sentence true.

Example A LIBRARY always has (posters, a carpet, <u>books</u>, DVDs, stairs).

11 A DUCK always has (a pond, bread, ducklings, webbed feet, a goose).

12 A SEA always has (boats, sand, shells, fish, water).

13 A TELEVISION always has (a screen, films, sport, wildlife, a stand).

14 An AQUARIUM always has (tropical fish, rocks, sharks, seaweed, glass).

15 A DICTIONARY always has (words, a hard cover, pictures, a bookshelf, a reader).

5

Underline the word in each line that uses three vowels.

16 appear	hounds	rotund	bitten	parcel
17 anchor	barrow	garage	prunes	street
18 specks	pulley	pocket	arrows	around
19 spirit	beaker	flight	errand	worthy
20 ferret	choose	gourds	plucky	tremor

5

If the code for GRANTS is d w h p m b, what do the following codes stand for?

21 w h d b _____

22 b m h w m _____

23 d w h b b _____

If the code for SPLASH is 5 9 2 3 5 0, what are the codes for the following words?

24 LASH _____

25 SLAP _____

5

In the changing room at the swimming pool there are twenty pegs in two equal rows. Number 1 is opposite 11, number 2 is opposite 12, and so on.

A group of six boys were the only ones in the changing room. From the information, work out who used each peg.

Raj hung his clothes on peg 16. Tom used the peg opposite Raj. Conan hung his clothes two pegs lower than Tom. Simon hung his clothes opposite Bert's. Simon's peg was four higher than Tom's and two higher than Marius'.

26 Tom used peg _____.

27 Conan used peg _____.

28 Simon used peg _____.

29 Bert used peg _____.

30 Marius used peg _____.

5

Find the missing letters and/or numbers. The alphabet has been written out to help you.

A B C D E F G H I J K L M N O P Q R S T U V W X Y Z

Example   AB is to CD as PQ is to <u>RS</u>.

31 RQ is to PO as HG is to ___.

32 GI is to KM as OQ is to ___.

33 FF is to HH as JJ is to ___.

34 M3 is to N4 as R8 is to ___.

35 HF is to DB as TR is to ___.

⑤ 5

Answer these alphabet questions.

A B C D E F G H I J K L M N O P Q R S T U V W X Y Z

36 If the letters of AUTUMN are put in alphabetical order, which comes third?   _____

37 Which month of the year begins with the fourteenth letter of the alphabet?   _____

38 Which month of the year ends with the twelfth letter?   _____

39 If the letters of the month DECEMBER are put in alphabetical order, which letter comes fourth?   _____

40 If the days of the week are put in alphabetical order, which comes sixth?   _____

○ 5

Find the three-letter word that can be added to the letters in capitals to make a new word. The new word will complete the sentence sensibly.

Example   The cat sprang onto the MO.   <u>USE</u>

41 I am FING these clothes before I put them away.   _____

42 Fabrice cut his GER badly on some broken glass.   _____

43 She had undone all the TONS on her cardigan.   _____

44 She does most of her shopping at the MET.   _____

45 He put his letter into an ENVEE and wrote the address. _____

○ 5

Focus test 1

1. bears
2. every
3. queen
4. name
5. bark
6. fill
7. deep
8. best
9. hint
10. lorry
11. G
12. 22
13. V
14. 3
15. February
16. Monday
17. spring
18. Friday
19. Saturday
20. L
21. I
22. L
23. R
24. H
25. fade
26. beef
27. deaf
28. hurries
29. mailed
30. excited

Focus test 2

1. high — low
2. young — old
3. strength — weakness
4. summer — winter
5. similar — different
6. enormous — huge
7. danger — peril
8. finish — end
9. light — pale
10. leave — depart
11. rock, stone
12. pretty, beautiful
13. certain, sure
14. jump, leap
15. under, beneath
16. empty, full
17. forwards, backwards
18. light, dark
19. public, private
20. simple, difficult

21. weary
22. remain
23. nasty
24. share
25. one
26. pull
27. sweet
28. take
29. rough
30. dark

Focus test 3

1. B — A
2. A — B
3. A — A
4. C — C
5. C — B
6. house — curtain
7. question — answer
8. table — engine
9. diamond — ruby
10. word — letter
11. main — baby
12. seek — hide
13. road — cross
14. trees — leaves
15. like — you

16.
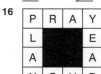

P	R	A	Y
L			E
A			A
Y	O	U	R

17.

B	I	T	E
A			V
S			I
H	E	E	L

18.

G	O	N	E
A		E	
M	E	A	T
E		R	

19.

	L		S
B	A	R	N
	V		A
P	A	N	G

Focus test 4

20.

J	O	K	E
E			A
E			S
P	I	T	Y

21. lunch — music
22. please — pencil
23. four — twelve
24. start — morning
25. would — house
26. POST — STOP
27. NEST — SENT
28. TALE — LATE
29. LOAF — FOAL
30. STEW — WEST

Focus test 4

1. CLOCK
2. TRAIN
3. OCTOPUS
4. TRAFFIC
5. BUTTER
6. FOOTBALL
7. f
8. w
9. c
10. s
11. b
12. g
13. r
14. k
15. f
16. t
17. y
18. k
19. SOON
20. BURN
21. BUST
22. SWORD
23. YEARLY
24. SCARF
25. CAT
26. FURY
27. ROT
28. ONE
29. FAIL
30. SHIN

Focus test 5

1. ironed — dress
   well
2. chicken — farm
   eggs

3. over — grazed
   knee
4. sun — hills
   dark
5. river — under
   bridge
6. Wednesday
   day — Tuesday
7. seat
8. water
9. buildings
10. ears
11. pupils
12. trees
13. workshop
14. flowerpot
15. someone
16. breakfast
17. message
18. leapfrog
19. toe
20. tab
21. drip
22. shed
23. mole
24. skin
25. rub
26. sir
27. eve
28. rage
29. dash
30. club

Focus test 6

1. bright — dark
2. poison — milk
3. vegetables — flowers
4. cinema — airport
5. bedroom — kitchen
6. LIP
7. PUT
8. TEN
9. ACE
10. ASK
11. black
12. bed
13. wind
14. green
15. foot
16. mount
17. warm
18. part
19. sticks
20. ice
21. BEEN

22	SLAP
23	NEXT
24	AREA
25	DARN
26	FARM
27	BORN
28	LIFE
29	WEED
30	SHIP

Focus test 7

1	9 3 5	
2	8 3 9 5	
3	SAME	
4	BUS	
5	SHE	
6	HUSH	
7	+ × −	
8	J H F	
9	M J H H P	
10	M J H O	
11	M J Z Q Q	
12	F J Z M	
13	small	fat
14	cow	dog
15	head	chin
16	wet	warm
17	LM	
18	P6	
19	MO	
20	TS	
21	E5	F6
22	LL	MM
23	NM	KJ
24	ZH	YI
25	LN	MM
26	EV	FW
27	11	9
28	15	25
29	33	18
30	16	26

Focus test 8

1	12
2	7
3	6
4	6
5	7
6	10
7	14
8	11
9	poodle
10	spaniel

11	labrador
12	collie
13	4
14	yellow
15	17
16	Jane
17	45 minutes
18	16:15
19	09:50
20	5
21	14
22	16
23	15
24	37
25	Friday
26	Sunday
27	Wednesday
28	£1.20
29	£1.70
30	5

Mixed paper 1

1	ocean	
2	garage	
3	dare	
4	peel	
5	cent	
6	13	16
7	7	3
8	11	19
9	19	10
10	33	55
11	jumped	swam
12	flower	tree
13	legs	wings
14	dry	wet
15	February	December
16	14	
17	3	
18	10	
19	6	
20	11	
21	top	bottom
22	left	right
23	little	large
24	dry	wet
25	high	low
26	parents prams	babies
27	hospital duty	nurses
28	biscuits table	plate
29	river side	boat

30	mother tea	cake
31	1	3
32	2	2
33	1	1
34	2	1
35	3	3
36	WHEELS	
37	ENGINE	
38	EIGHT	
39	PENCILS	
40	LEMON	
41	boring	
42	border	
43	entertain	
44	accurate	
45	healthy	

Mixed paper 2

1	a	
2	s	
3	c	
4	g	
5	p	
6	HIM	
7	FOR	
8	FEE	
9	ARC	
10	TEN	
11	window	plate
12	basket	foot
13	sit	stand
14	juice	fly
15	ring	service
16	TAME	
17	MAST	
18	THEM	
19	2 5 1 4	
20	7 3 5 1	
21	first	
22	billow	
23	berry	
24	chimp	
25	boost	
26	skinny, thin	
27	quick, fast	
28	flat, even	
29	beautiful, attractive	
30	weak, feeble	
31	glass	
32	ingredients	
33	fingers	
34	stone	
35	hooves	

36	14
37	19
38	17
39	16
40	21
41	base
42	rung
43	scan
44	fury
45	suit

Mixed paper 3

1	t	
2	g	
3	n	
4	k	
5	h	
6	alter	change
7	heat	warmth
8	choose	pick
9	precious	valuable
10	eager	keen
11	school	
12	post	
13	up	
14	hand	
15	cart	
16	B	
17	D	
18	A	
19	C	
20	C	
21	M	
22	K	

23

F	O	O	D
U		W	
L	I	L	T
L		S	

24

K	I	N	G
I			N
L			A
N	E	A	T

25

H	E	A	P
	C		O
T	H	I	S
	O		T

26 f g d w

Column 1

27 v g p d
28 d w p v
29 BAKE
30 BEAK
31 D
32 G
33 23
34 X
35 L
36 <u>watching</u> <u>frightening</u>
37 <u>wall</u> <u>picture</u>
38 <u>house</u> <u>week</u>
39 <u>very</u> <u>four</u>
40 <u>after</u> <u>to</u>
41 fireproof
42 scrapbook
43 carpet
44 fingerprint
45 belong

Mixed paper 4

1 December
2 Friday
3 autumn
4 Wednesday
5 Sunday
6 CLEVER
7 START
8 WHEAT
9 SCREAM
10 SPINE
11 deer
12 noun
13 pest
14 south
15 rice
16 track
17 her
18 find
19 rain
20 steel
21 laugh, cry
22 clean, dirty
23 alive, dead
24 rude, polite
25 tick, cross
26 14
27 5
28 6
29 5
30 2
31 GIRAFFE
32 COLLAR

Column 2

33 ELEVEN
34 DOCTOR
35 STREET

36

W	O	R	M
O	■	■	O
R	■	■	O
K	I	N	D

37

S	T	O	P
■	W	■	A
L	I	A	R
■	N	■	K

38

M	I	N	D
A	■	■	U
S	■	■	S
T	O	O	K

39

F	■	■	H
I	D	L	E
L	■	■	R
L	O	V	E

40

B	E	L	T
E	■	■	O
E	■	■	U
F	O	U	R

41 ABLE
42 LAST
43 LATE
44 ? < £ *
45 > < £ ?

Mixed paper 5

1 7
2 horses
3 4
4 3
5 Class 1
6 looked found
7 fought battle
8 mother table
9 green garage
10 rabbit hutch
11 easy
12 busy
13 scowl

Column 3

14 ancient
15 deserve
16 EVER
17 POND
18 LAME
19 ROCK
20 FAME
21 1 3 3 2
22 1 4 9 6
23 1 3 5
24 2 8 1 2 7
25 4 7 2
26 M
27 S
28 N
29 O
30 G
31 14   23
32 99   55
33 3   7
34 55   50
35 13   11
36 peas
37 loom
38 lice
39 hose
40 sets
41 VEIN
42 LAZY
43 FIRE
44 FILM
45 PATH

Mixed paper 6

1 LAID DIAL
2 MADE DAME
3 SORE ROSE
4 DUSTY STUDY
5 SPORE ROPES
6 1
7 2
8 4
9 2
10 3
11 40 minutes
12 09:20
13 11:00
14 75 minutes
15 09:45
16 face
17 dead
18 bead
19 cede
20 café

Column 4

21 ROOM
22 PACK
23 MINT
24 BONE
25 HARD
26 stream lane
27 green blue
28 sad pretty
29 glove sock
30 train plane

31

Y	O	U	R
■	N	■	U
P	L	U	S
■	Y	■	H

32

B	A	R	K
O	■	■	I
U	■	■	S
T	H	I	S

33 back
34 open
35 love
36 further
37 worse
38 9 1 6 6 5
39 9 0 4
40 4 1 6 7 0
41 2 3 6 6 5
42 7 1 6 0
43 haircut
44 prepare
45 elastic

Mixed paper 7

1 BELT
2 MADE
3 MEET
4 BITE
5 HUMP
6 <u>cliffs</u> <u>nests</u>
7 <u>you</u> <u>your</u>
8 <u>chain</u> <u>bicycle</u>
9 <u>twelve</u> <u>midday</u>
10 <u>two</u> <u>some</u>
11 webbed feet
12 water
13 a screen
14 glass
15 words
16 appear
17 garage

18 around
19 beaker
20 choose
21 RAGS
22 START
23 GRASS
24 2 3 5 0
25 5 2 3 9
26 6
27 4
28 10
29 20
30 8
31 FE
32 SU
33 LL
34 S9
35 PN
36 N
37 November
38 April

39 E
40 Tuesday
41 OLD
42 FIN
43 BUT
44 ARK
45 LOP

Mixed paper 8

1 CJ   HV
2 CC   EE
3 I9   K8
4 RS   UV
5 TS   RQ
6 sane
7 tan
8 tile
9 on
10 put
11 book   exciting
    down

12 broke   window
    balls
13 custard   cream
    pudding
14 hot   plants
    fields
15 runners   thirsty
    end
16 B
17 E
18 small
19 yes
20 big
21 children   pillow
22 twenty   hours
23 times   woolly
24 camera   pond
25 clouds   gloomy
26 Wednesday
27 Friday
28 Monday
29 45

30 35
31 pig   cow
32 slow   soft
33 rocket   train
34 shallow   short
35 male   lake
36 l
37 c
38 m
39 g
40 w
41 EACH
42 KITE
43 WANE
44 DUTY
45 FINE

Mixed paper 8

Find the two missing pairs of letters and/or numbers in the following sequences. The alphabet has been written out to help you.

A B C D E F G H I J K L M N O P Q R S T U V W X Y Z

Example	CQ	DP	EQ	FP	GQ	HP
1	___	DV	EJ	FV	GJ	___
2	BB	___	DD	___	FF	GG
3	C8	E9	G8	___	___	M9
4	PQ	QR	___	ST	TU	___
5	___	___	PO	NM	LK	JI

5

Change the first word of the third pair in the same way as the other pairs to give a new word.

Example	bind, hind	bare, hare	but, hut
6	flame, same	brave, save	crane, _____
7	win, tin	won, ton	wan, _____
8	milk, mile	film, file	tilt, _____
9	grit, it	into, to	soon, _____
10	beat, bat	flat, fat	pout, _____

5

Complete the following sentences by selecting the most sensible word from each group of words given in the brackets. Underline the words selected.

Example The (<u>children</u>, boxes, foxes) carried the (houses, <u>books</u>, steps) home from the (greengrocer, <u>library</u>, factory).

11 Her (book, shirt, branch) was so (green, exciting, kind), she could not put it (down, up, through).

12 Mac (broke, ate, hung) the kitchen (moon, pond, window) with one of his tennis (stones, nets, balls).

13 Would you like (ketchup, yellow, custard) or (gravy, vinegar, cream) with your (pudding, bowl, plate)?

14 It is so (hot, pink, deep) the (plants, flames, biscuits) are withering and dying in the (fields, bath, grapes).

15 The (runners, sticks, houses) were tired and (marked, bitten, thirsty) by the (beginning, end, inside) of the marathon.

5

There are five presents waiting for Angie to open them.
Present A, Present B and Present C are big.
Present D and Present E are small.
Present A, Present C and Present E are wrapped in boxes.
Present C and Present B are in paper with balloons on.
Present E and Present D are wrapped in silver paper.
The remaining present is wrapped in paper with Happy Birthday written on it.

16 Which present is not boxed and is covered in balloon paper? _____

17 Which present is silver and box shaped? _____

18 Is this present big or small? _____

19 Is the Happy Birthday paper on a box? _____

20 Is this present big or small? _____

5

Rearrange the muddled words in capital letters so that each sentence makes sense.

Example There are sixty SNODCES _seconds_ in a UTMINE _minute_.

21 At bedtime, the DRENHILC _____ had a LOPIWL _____ fight.

22 There are WNYTTE _____ -four RUHSO _____ in a day.

23 In prehistoric MESTI _____, LOLOWY _____ mammoths roamed the land.

24 By mistake, I dropped my MERACA _____ in the DPNO _____.

25 The DLCOUS _____ have turned the sky grey and LOMOGY _____.

5

If yesterday was Tuesday, answer these questions.

26 Which day of the week was it a week ago from today? _____

27 What is the day after tomorrow? _____

28 What is the day two days ago from today? _____

3

It is feeding time at the zoo in the gorilla area. The mother gorilla has 10 pieces of fruit more than the youngster, who has 25 fewer pieces than the silver-backed father. He has 60 pieces of fruit.

29 How many pieces of fruit does the mother gorilla have? _____

30 How many pieces of fruit does the young gorilla have? _____   2

Complete the following sentences in the best way by choosing one word from each set of brackets.

Example Tall is to (tree, <u>short</u>, colour) as narrow is to (thin, white, <u>wide</u>).

31 Pork is to (sheep, pig, chicken) as beef is to (cow, swan, lion).

32 Quick is to (slim, slip, slow) as hard is to (firm, difficult, soft).

33 Astronaut is to (rocket, memory, hill) as passenger is to (journey, train, station).

34 Deep is to (pool, gone, shallow) as tall is to (sky, top, short).

35 Lame is to (male, crow, file) as kale is to (pond, river, lake).   5

Find the letter that will end the first word and start the second word.

Example drow (<u>n</u>) ought

36 bel (__) ovely   **37** mimi (__) ome

38 sla (__) etre   **39** dra (__) arment

40 allo (__) ise   5

Look at the first group of three words. The word in the middle has been made from the two other words. Complete the second group of three words in the same way, making a new word in the middle.

Example	PAIN	<u>IN</u>TO	T<u>OO</u>K	ALSO	<u>SOON</u>	ONLY
41	EYES	YELL	FALL	HEAP	_____	ITCH
42	JAMS	SOLE	LOVE	BUNK	_____	TIME
43	SLOP	POUR	URGE	CLAW	_____	NEST
44	SEND	MALE	CLAM	TYRE	_____	STUD
45	WEEK	WEEP	COPY	FIND	_____	TIER

5